Books by Linda J. Williams

Church Etiquette: A Handbook for Manners and Appropriate Behavior in Church

Church Etiquette:

A Handbook for Doorkeepers

LINDA J. WILLIAMS

WESTBOW·
PRESS
A DIVISION OF THOMAS NELSON
& ZONDERVAN

All Scripture quotations and scriptures provided in this book, unless
otherwise indicated, are taken from The Holy Bible in the King James
Version, Thomas Nelson Publishers (1984, 1977), Nashville, TN.

WestBow Press books may be ordered through
booksellers or by contacting:

WestBow Press
A Division of Thomas Nelson & Zondervan
1663 Liberty Drive
Bloomington, IN 47403
www.westbowpress.com
1 (866) 928-1240

ISBN: 978-1-4908-7268-1 (sc)
ISBN: 978-1-4908-7269-8 (e)

Library of Congress Control Number: 2015903629

Print information available on the last page.

WestBow Press rev. date: 3/16/2015

Contents

Foreword...ix

Introduction...xiii

History of the Gatekeeper/Doorkeeper.......................1

Keeping the Door 10

Doorkeeper Leadership Roles 15

The Doorkeeper: Protocol in the Sanctuary.............. 19

Doorkeepers Preparing for Service............................ 26

Qualities of a Doorkeeper 29

Attitude of a Doorkeeper 36

The Spirit of Hospitality 41

Goals for Growth 45

The Passion to Be a Doorkeeper................................ 49

All thanksgiving and glory to God for the spiritual gift of writing. To Pastor Victor J. Lewis for his obedience to God in leading and guiding me to cultivate the gifts that God has deposited in me. To my husband, Henry Williams, for his love and patience, and for his input and insight as a doorkeeper. To my sister, Ruby Dixon, for her encouragement and her insight as an usher. In memory of my late sister, Saundra Oliver (Pookie), whose trust, faith, and obedience to God exemplified a godly life and inspired me to have courage and trust God. To my children, Jonathan and Tiffany, for their encouragement and support.

Foreword

If you are holding this book, then you realize that there is some information about the approach to worship from the very sanctuary doors that you desire to learn or at least gain insight about. The Word of God is clear that there is a divine way to approach the Lord, and it is my fervent belief that the closer you adhere to those instructions, the more likely you will be to make it right into His divine presence, the very throne room of God. We in the faith must acknowledge that this worship experience begins at the sanctuary doors.

Unfortunately, the Christian faith is being driven by the tenets of tradition and culture rather than the Word of God. This nouveau approach to our ancient faith is negatively impacting the worship and operations of the church more than any church, pastor, or leader is willing to admit, and all for the sake of comfort. Those of us who are witnessing the comfort of the saints of God in this season would agree that there is always a remnant of those who refuse to settle or conform to the ways of the world.

It is in the midst of these challenges that we can be encouraged by the fact that one of the few unwavering and uncompromising soldiers on the battlefield for the cause of Christ is Sister Linda J. Williams. Her works are not for the faint of heart. If you are not of a *sola scriptura* (Latin for "the Word alone") mind-set, then it is probably best that you close this book and don't journey any farther through the pages of hardline truths that are about to be biblically presented to you. I dare say that to continue pressing forward (especially if you are in the leadership of the church) is to risk the conviction that will come Sunday after Sunday because you have been enlightened by the information presented to you. At some point, you may be compelled by the Holy Spirit to act upon what you know to be relevant truth.

As with most ministerial gifts and callings, this book was birthed out of the pain and discomfort of looking through a biblical lens at one of the traditional auxiliaries of the church in light of the Word of God and making a determination as to whether we will continue to please man or demolish what was in existence and elevate to the height of our priorities an obedience to God and His Word. We prayed and fasted and chose the latter, not for us but all for the glory of God.

This book, along with many others that are being written during this season, has been written to address the void of quality instruction and materials that should be in place as a resource for new pastors, church leaders, et al. I am grateful to God that this void has been filled, and I am confident that the Lord is going to use Sister Linda J. Williams' gift to author many more books to bridge the gap of biblical truth versus church tradition.

Pastor Victor J. Lewis
Friendship Missionary Baptist Church,
Roslyn Heights, New York

Introduction

If you stand at the doors of your church to let worshippers in and out, assist in keeping order and decency in the sanctuary, or desire a better understanding of the job of those who stand at the doors of the sanctuary, this book is for you. These pages provide important information regarding the role of a doorkeeper as outlined in the Word of God.

The focus of this book is on the spiritual quality and courteous behavior that doorkeepers should possess if they are to be effective. Some instructional rules are discussed, but this book uniquely connects the rules of courtesy with the responsibilities of a doorkeeper. Implementing the rules and responsibilities of a doorkeeper without having a courteous spirit may lead to misunderstandings and conflict.

As a certified etiquette consultant, I have devoted the past thirteen years of my life to training others in the area of appropriate behavior. Once God revealed to me that the focus of my purpose and gift was in the area of Christian courtesy, I asked God to lead me in the areas in which He would have me to focus. When I was asked to put together a training manual for the doorkeepers in our church, I knew that being a doorkeeper was not my gift! This was revealed to me as God led me to spend time at the door to experience the duties of a doorkeeper before writing the training manual. I spent much time in prayer, meditation, and study of the Word while writing the training manual. My brief experience on the door together with the input from other doorkeepers/ushers contributed to the information in this book. I was also guided by direction of the Holy Spirit in the area of spiritual courtesy as it relates to those who stand at the door. The information in these pages provides a blueprint for the way to become a more focused, caring, and spirit-filled doorkeeper.

I believe that this book was divinely inspired. It was only by the Spirit of God that my pastor decided to restructure and have men as doorkeepers stand at the door instead of ushers. As etiquette officer he asked me to do research, develop a training manual and facilitate the training. Although I was hesitant to do the training, I agreed that I would do it. I learned a long time ago that when you are asked to do something in the kingdom of God, especially by your pastor, you prayerfully take the assignment. First, the Holy Spirit revealed that, in order to train someone, you must have some experience in the area in which you will train. I understood that I must stand at the doors to better understand the position. I knew that it was a difficult job, but I had no idea how difficult. Even the former ushers gave me some tips, but it was still a difficult task. After the training and research was completed, my pastor shared with me that I should publish the manual as a handbook. He felt that it would be useful for churches of all sizes and denominations to assist their doorkeepers/ushers. Then I understood why I had been asked to put the manual together: it provides the unique basis for this book.

While researching currently published books on ushers for the training, I found only one that briefly connected the historical doorkeeper with the modern usher, but not in the depth that I was seeking. In order to provide the training that I felt was necessary for our new doorkeepers, I had to put together a more exhaustive manual, with some reference material as well as my expertise in the area of appropriate behavior.

As you read this book, you will find that it connects the role of the doorkeeper in the Old Testament with the role of the doorkeeper/usher of today. This book is different in that it brings the aspect of church etiquette and courtesy as an important quality of being a doorkeeper. The etiquette component is mentioned because is an integral part of the book in the development of the character of the doorkeeper.

The book begins with the biblical history of the doorkeeper. You must have a foundational biblical understanding of the role before we can understand how this role transitions to modern day doorkeepers, so don't allow the first chapter to discourage you from reading further. The characteristics of a doorkeeper are also discussed, as well as the responsibilities. The information provided can be applied to doorkeepers at all churches. This book provides information that will attempt to bridge the character gap between the Old Testament doorkeepers and the contemporary doorkeeper to develop a doorkeeper who is both God centered and a willing servant to the worshippers of today's church.

The information provided in this book must be reviewed prayerfully. You may feel that some material is redundant, but the information in each chapter is connected and information is repeated for emphasis as needed. You may feel that the character described for the doorkeeper is too rigid. The primary characteristics are courtesy, which is a behavior and not an emotion, and a spirit of discernment, which comes from God. All jobs and positions should have a job description, and the doorkeeper should be no different. I encourage you to read through the whole book just to gain what may be a different perspective of the job of a doorkeeper, even if you are not a doorkeeper/usher.

As you read, keep in mind that all churches have different rules governing the protocol of their church. General denominational rules may be the same, but because there are different people in every church, there may be some variations to rules in every church.

You cannot discuss the job description of a doorkeeper without discussing the rules of your church, because it is the doorkeeper's job to make sure those rules are followed. It is not my intention to promote changing the rules but to spark a discussion regarding the relevance of current rules and guidelines. For clarification purposes, the words *doorkeeper, gatekeeper,* and *usher,* when used in this book, will be synonymous.

It is my prayer that the information in this book prompts a change in your church protocol that results in a more courteous and orderly atmosphere. If that happens, my prayers have been answered.

CHAPTER ONE

History of the Gatekeeper/ Doorkeeper

The following is a synopsis of the origin of the role of the doorkeeper in the Old Testament times:

Shallum, son of Kore in the Old Testament, had been in charge of a gate some forty years before the temple's destruction, now he led the entire crew of gatekeepers[1].

In Psalm 84:10, the psalmist says, "for a day in thy courts is better than a thousand. I had rather be a doorkeeper in the house of my God, than to dwell in the tents of wickedness[2]."

---

[1] Hendrickson Publishers Marketing (1991, 2008). Matthew Henry's Commentary on the Whole Bible. Hendrickson Publishers Marketing, Peabody, MA.

[2] Thomas Nelson Publishers (1984, 1977) The Holy Bible in the King James Version. Thomas Nelson Publishers, Nashville, TN

Thomas Nelson Publishers (1984, 1977) The Holy Bible in the King James Version. Thomas Nelson Publishers, Nashville, TN

1

In biblical times, persons were appointed to keep the street door leading into the interior of the house. The Scriptures show that doorkeepers could be female. John 18:16 states,

> But Peter stood at the door without. Then
> went out that other disciple, which was known
> unto the high priest, and spake unto her that
> kept the door, and brought in Peter[3].

Most of the Scriptures referring to doorkeepers/ gatekeepers indicate that this position was held by males. I would imagine that these individuals were primarily male due to the minimal leadership and official roles held by women in the church during that time. There was also the potential of having to defend the doors or gate from physical attack or battle. Doorkeepers/gatekeepers also received collections from the people (2 Kings 22:4).

> Go up to Hilkiah the high priest, that he
> may sum the silver which is brought into
> the house of the Lord, which the keepers of
> the door have gathered of the people[4].

---

[3] Thomas Nelson Publishers (1984, 1977) The Holy Bible in the King James Version. Thomas Nelson Publishers, Nashville, TN

[4] Thomas Nelson Publishers (1984, 1977) The Holy Bible in the King James Version. Thomas Nelson Publishers, Nashville, TN

First Chronicles 9:19 says,

> And Shallum the son of Kore, the son of
> Ebiasaph, the son of Korah, and his brethren, of
> the house of his father, the Korahites, were over
> the work of the service, keepers of the gates of
> the tabernacle: and their fathers, being over the
> host of the Lord, were keepers of the entry[5].

They were responsible for guarding the entrance to
the dwelling of the Lord.

> "Many of the Levites were employed as porters of the
> gates of the House of God. They had the oversight
> of the gates, and were keepers of the thresholds, and
> keepers of the entry. This seemed a mean office, and
> yet David would rather have it *than dwell in the tents
> of wickedness* (Psalms 84:10). Their office was to; 1.
> Open the doors of God's house every morning, and
> shut them every night, 2. To keep off the unclean and
> hinder those from thrusting that were forbidden by
> law, 3. To direct and introduce into the courts of the
> Lord those that came thither to worship and to show
> them where to go and what to do that they might not

---

[5] Thomas Nelson Publishers (1984, 1977) The Holy Bible in the
King James Version. Thomas Nelson Publishers, Nashville, TN

incur punishment. This required care and diligence and constant attendance[6]."

The position of a doorkeeper has always been one of great importance and held in high esteem. People in biblical times didn't just decide to become doorkeepers; they were appointed based on their past positions and experiences. The descendants of Judah—Shallum, Akkub, Talmon, Ahiman, and their relatives—were chosen as gatekeepers after their return to Israel from exile. Please read the ninth chapter of 1 Chronicles to fully understand the appointment of the first doorkeepers/gatekeepers.

A doorkeeper's job was to protect the entrance to the temple, serve the people, and create an atmosphere of order and hospitality. It was not a position to be taken lightly. Today in our country, we have men and women at our doors who are usually called ushers. Ushers are modern-day doorkeepers or gatekeepers for the house of the Lord.

Ushers are people-centered, doorkeepers
are God-Centered[7].

---

[6] Hendrickson Publishers Marketing (1991, 2008). Matthew Henry's Commentary on the Whole Bible. Hendricks Publishers Marketing, Peabody, MA.

[7] Parrott, L (2002) Serving as a Church Usher. Zondervan, Grand Rapids, MI.

The duties of today's doorkeepers are to stand inside the sanctuary doors, to serve worshippers, and to maintain order.

The Scriptures indicate that doorkeepers/gatekeepers in biblical times were God centered. Their primary duty was keeping the laws of the sanctuary according to the rules established by the priests. Their secondary duty was to the people who came to worship, to see to their comfort. When we observe ushers performing their duties today, extraordinary emphasis is placed on the comfort of the pastor and the members and less emphasis on enforcing, or even creating, rules of the sanctuary. It is a more difficult job today for many reasons. The availability of cell phones, iPads, undisciplined children, and belligerent adults can make a doorkeeper's job much more challenging and demanding than during biblical times. Doorkeepers battle in a different way in today's churches. They must be mindful not to discourage someone who may be seeking a church home by reprimanding them for inappropriate behavior in the sanctuary. At the same time, they have a job to do: to maintain order, decency, and respect for God's sanctuary at all times.

Today's individuals who stand at the church doors must be a combination of doorkeeper, gatekeeper, counselor, disciplinarian, and hospitality representative with all of the duties and responsibilities required of each position. They are also the representative of the church as they are usually the first person that people meet as they come through the doors of the sanctuary.

It is a peculiar job and takes a specific character to accomplish this task. The following are some of the roles that describe today's doorkeeper:

Encourager—Those who attend the door in the church render a service to God and to those who enter, which plays an important part in the worship service. They can be a positive difference in someone's life or a light in the midst of their darkness.

Disciplinarian—Those who attend the door must make sure that an atmosphere of reverence and order is maintained before, during, and after the service. Their motivation for maintaining this atmosphere must be God centered. When you show worshippers to their seats, you do so with kindness and a spirit of hospitality for God. If they give you resistance, you must still treat them with love. Doorkeepers must have the right attitude toward their work and have a godly spirit. Without it, they may do more harm than good. If your attitude causes a person to leave the church, what have you accomplished for the Lord?

Maintainer of a Spirit of Worship—"But the Lord is in His holy temple: let all the earth keep silence before Him (Habakkuk 2:20)[8]." If someone is being disruptive during the service, it is the doorkeeper's duty to assist

---

[8] Thomas Nelson Publishers (1984, 1977) The Holy Bible in the King James Version. Thomas Nelson Publishers, Nashville, TN

in maintaining order. Ask disruptive people if you can help them with something. If there is no problem, kindly (with a smile) ask them to keep their conversation to a minimum out of respect for others and in reverence to the Spirit of God.

Maintainer of Order and Decency—(1 Corinthians 14:40) The presence of the Spirit of God in the sanctuary requires an atmosphere of reverence and respect. People must conduct themselves according to the rules of the sanctuary, which they must be taught. Doorkeepers are to maintain the atmosphere of reverence and respect, but it must be done in a loving and kind manner.

Host for God—Doorkeepers acts as hosts for God, as the official welcoming personnel of the house of the Lord. Doorkeepers must also look after the comforts and needs of all of the worshippers in the church. For visitors, it also means not making them feel awkward or left out. Make sure they have Bibles, hymnbooks, and programs, as well as copies of any church creed or mission statement that may be recited during the service. Introduce them to other members if possible, especially if they are alone and you are seating them. This may not be possible, of course, if they arrive after service has begun.

Evangelist—One of the Dictionary.com definitions of evangelism is "missionary zeal, purpose, or activity." As doorkeepers, when greeting those who come into the church, pay attention to their demeanor and facial expressions. They may need an extra smile or a hug. Once they are in the church it is your job to discern their needs whether it's a loving smile, assistance, or prayer. The purpose of being attentive is to make all feel welcome. Our primary purpose as Christians is to lead souls to Christ and to glorify God. By having the attitude of an evangelist while at the door, you may very well be fulfilling both of these purposes.

Public Relations Representative—Visitors receive their first impression of the church from the doorkeepers. One of the purposes of the doorkeeper is to convey a favorable impression to those who come in—to make the person feel that people in the church care about them and that the members are kind and friendly.

Humble Servant—The doorkeeper is an important person in the Lord's work. He/she should be honored that they have been chosen by God to do this work and be enthusiastic about the position for which they have been chosen. It is a great honor to be a doorkeeper, but a doorkeeper must be a person with a humble spirit.

Notes on History of the Gatekeeper/Doorkeeper

_____

_____

_____

_____

_____

_____

_____

_____

_____

_____

_____

_____

_____

_____

_____

_____

_____

_____

_____

_____

_____

_____

_____

_____

_____

CHAPTER TWO

Keeping the Door

My personal belief is that you should never write about a topic for which you do have not have knowledge or some experience. The purpose of a handbook is to share knowledge and provide information for improvement on a topic. How can you share what you have not experienced?

I continue to emphasize that being a doorkeeper is not easy! It is a gift and a ministry for those who do it. Watching those who stand at the door is much easier than standing at the door. Those who are good at their job make it look easy, but I tell you from personal experience that it is not easy. One of the most difficult parts for me was focusing on several different areas of the sanctuary at the same time. I liked being able to greet all who came through the door because that is my personality. I always managed to get a smile from even the gruffest individuals. Whether you know it or not, a smile is infectious. When people walk through the doors of the sanctuary, we never know the struggle that they went through to make it to church. Our struggle, as doorkeepers, must be put aside for those who come to the houses of worship. We have made a commitment and been appointed to stand at the door of the church. We are to be servants and beacons of light to all who come in.

Those of you who have been standing at the door for years may think that standing at the door for several weeks did not provide enough education for me on the trials and tests that a doorkeeper endures. Perhaps you are correct, but believe me: I walked away with a whole new perspective, appreciation, and respect for those who stand at the door! During those weeks at the door, I found that people can be rude, insulting, demanding, selfish, and very un-Christ like. Some people do not know the rules of the sanctuary; others just disregard the rules and do what they want. Some people expect the doorkeepers to cater to their every need, regardless of how rude *they* may be, and do it without a frown or complaint! Honestly, that *is* our mandate: to be a servant to those who walk through the doors of the sanctuary. It is a serious commitment, one that cannot be taken lightly. If you are not ready to be criticized, spoken to rudely, or talked about for your efforts to keep order, you are not ready to be a doorkeeper. By the way, you must take on all of the negativity in the previous sentence and do so with the genuine love of God on your face and in your heart! If we respond in the same way that we are treated, we may push people out of the church and away from God. We must, instead, treat others the way we want to be treated.

Being a doorkeeper can be extremely challenging. You must constantly be alert to the pastor as well as the members and guests in the sanctuary. You must be looking everywhere at once and be ready to move at a moment's notice. You must move quickly, quietly, and inconspicuously. You must keep your composure at all times while enforcing the rules of the sanctuary. You must constantly listen for God's direction, because sometimes you will see someone doing something out of order but the Holy Spirit will say, "Don't say anything to them."

People expect to receive the gift of a smile when they walk through the church doors. We want to let them know that, regardless of whatever they had been through before they entered those doors, they are entering the house of the Lord and will find love and peace within those walls.

Your primary responsibility as a doorkeeper is to keep order and decency in the sanctuary so that the move of the Spirit will not be quenched and those who walk through the doors will feel the Spirit of the Lord and receive the word that God has for them. You are also expected to extend the spirit of hospitality to all who enter the doors by doing all that you can to make them comfortable and welcome. This means that you should anticipate people's needs before they even ask. Be aware of what is going on in the church at all times, and be ready to assist whenever necessary in a courteous, spiritual, and expert manner. It is the role of a military officer and a hotel concierge intertwined by the Holy Spirit. Your speech and actions must be guided by the Holy Spirit so that you can be spiritually guided for what needs to be said or done at any given moment. *Your role is the role of a servant.*

I will end this chapter with scriptures I found regarding loving your neighbor (remember that everyone is considered your neighbor). I am sure there are many more, but these will help you to know that this is one of God's greatest commandments: Leviticus 19:18, 34; Matthew 7:12; Matthews 19:19; Mathew 22:39; Luke 6:31; Romans 13:9; Galatians 5:14; and James 2:8.

Notes on Keeping the Door

_____

_____

_____

_____

_____

_____

_____

_____

_____

_____

_____

_____

_____

_____

_____

_____

_____

_____

_____

_____

_____

_____

_____

_____

_____

_____

_____

CHAPTER THREE

Doorkeeper Leadership Roles

Doorkeeper roles can vary depending on the church and the duties assigned. It can encompass some or all of the positions below. The roles are dependent upon the size of your church, the number of persons available to stand at the door, and your pastor's or administrative board's vision for your doorkeeper roles. My purpose in providing this information is to summarize some of the duties that may be assigned to those who stand at the door.

Head Doorkeeper—has the responsible position of manager or executive. Head doorkeeper is in charge of the doorkeeper staff. This person must personally direct the staff at every church service, and if they cannot be present, they must see to it that the assistant doorkeeper or someone else takes their place. It is the responsibility of the head doorkeeper to enlist the other doorkeepers' assistance. He or she must consult with the pastor before a new doorkeeper is chosen, unless the pastor defers that authority to them. The head doorkeeper must be chosen carefully. This person must not only have the experience and knowledge required of one who stands at the door, they must possess strong leadership skills as well. It will be their job to create a schedule and make sure that the other doorkeepers adhere to the schedule. It should be a written schedule agreed to by all doorkeepers. If the head doorkeeper cannot be both an excellent keeper of the door and be a leader for the other doorkeepers to follow, the position should be reassigned to someone that can accomplish both of these roles. If the doorkeepers do not function properly, it affects the whole church.

Head doorkeepers must explain rules and regulations to all staff, new and existing. All doorkeepers must work together as one; they must be on one accord in all duties. They should review all rules and responsibilities with staff before they assume their duties. The head doorkeeper must be well versed in all duties for which doorkeepers are responsible. This will vary from church to church. Just because you are a doorkeeper/usher at one church does not mean that you know the rules and protocol at all churches. The head doorkeeper may want to create a checklist that can be given to each doorkeeper so that everyone understands his or her duties and what is expected. All assignments to individuals must be specific, and everyone should be aware of their individual duties and the duties of others so there is no conflict.

The head doorkeeper is responsible for making sure the correct number of personnel are on duty for each service. A schedule should be made and staff assigned on a rotating basis, if sufficient staff is available. New doorkeepers should not be paired together. They should be paired with a seasoned doorkeeper for training purposes. The head doorkeeper makes sure that all personnel are at their posts at the appointed time. Doorkeepers should pray together prior to going to their posts so that they are on one accord and focused on the work of the Lord.

Assistant to the Doorkeeper—if necessary, an assistant can be appointed. This person assists the doorkeeper as assignments are delegated. If the head doorkeeper is unable to attend a service or event, the assistant doorkeeper will step in to make sure all is in order.

Doorkeeper Staff—there are many roles for the doorkeeper. You may decide to designate a specific doorkeeper, who has their post near the pulpit, to the pastor. You may have a specific doorkeeper to tend to the needs of guest pastors. You may also decide that some doorkeepers are in charge of making sure the sanctuary is clean and has hymnals, Bibles, envelopes, etc., before service begins. This is especially important if you have more than one service.

The important thing to remember about the job description of the doorkeepers is that everyone should know the head doorkeeper and that they are the person in charge of making sure that the doorkeeper team runs smoothly. All members of the doorkeeper staff must be willing to work under the supervision of the head and assistant doorkeepers.

Notes on Doorkeeper Leadership Roles

_____
_____
_____
_____
_____
_____
_____
_____
_____
_____
_____
_____
_____
_____
_____
_____
_____
_____
_____
_____
_____
_____
_____
_____
_____
_____

CHAPTER FOUR

The Doorkeeper: Protocol in the Sanctuary

As etiquette officer of my church, my post is sitting in the last pew in the church. This allows me to see the behaviors and hear the conversations of the worshippers. With the aid of the Holy Spirit, I see situations that must be addressed before, during, and after service. Being in the back of the church, similar to being in the pulpit, gives you a full vantage point of the actions and behaviors of the individuals in the sanctuary.

People can be very rude when entering the sanctuary. Depending on what is going on, the doorkeeper may let them in and ask them to remain at the back of the church until instructed to take a seat. Sometimes, people do not follow instructions and head directly to a seat. This is inappropriate for two reasons. First, you are late. Second, it is disrespectful to enter the sanctuary during prayer, Scripture, praise, or any time in which you are asked to wait.

I give the above example because it illustrates the difficulty of being a doorkeeper. It takes a disciplined doorkeeper not to lose control in a situation such as the one described above. You must be able to handle this situation, and so many others, with love and respect for the other person. At the same time, you must enforce the rules of the sanctuary to keep order.

To enforce the rules of the sanctuary, you must know the rules. You must not only know the rules but also know why the rules are in place and be able to defend them when necessary. You must always be ready to explain the rules that you are enforcing. People may not agree with the reason for the rule, but they must respect that there is a rule in place. Even in our government, there are rules that we don't agree with, but we obey them because we know that it is the law and we must deal with the consequences of not obeying the law. If we are willing to obey laws and rules in the world, why would we not be willing to do the same in the church?

It is important that the head doorkeeper meet with the pastor to discuss the rules. If you do not know the reason for a rule or procedure, ask. If no one knows the reason for the rule, you should probably discuss whether that rule should still be in place or revised.

Many churches today have a code of conduct. It is a list of eight or ten rules to abide by in the sanctuary and is posted in a prominent place for all to see. Some churches include their code of conduct in their bulletins or programs. By posting the primary rules of respect for the sanctuary, worshippers will be able to see the rules and not wonder why they are being approached when they are breaking one of the rules. This should also prevent people from feeling offended when approached. Examples of the rules to be considered in the sanctuary are:

- whether or not food or drink of any kind is allowed in the sanctuary (including choir members who might need water when singing);
- turning off cell phones;
- whether or not attendees must stand for reading of the Scripture and prayer;
- where you can and cannot walk during service;
- when you can and cannot walk during service;
- entering the sanctuary;
- being instructed to follow the directions of the doorkeepers (ushers);
- protocol for movement during Scripture and prayer; and
- Instructions for communion.

Agreeing on the rules is one thing; enforcing them without offending others is quite another task. It takes a special personality to tell someone they are out of order in church and to do so with a spirit of love and kindness. When telling someone that they are violating a rule of the sanctuary, be sure to tell them what the rule is and why the rule is in place. This should be done quickly and quietly. Also, all doorkeepers must be on one accord when doing this. The primary reason is to respect God and His place of worship. When I was on the door, I found that because I spoke to people in a respectable tone and with a smile, in most cases, the correction was received positively. I also asked with a smile, not a frown (Job 9:27 Holman Christian Standard Bible). Sometimes, people will be offended that you spoke to them regarding their behavior no matter how polite you are when speaking to them. Those are the people you speak to about their behavior as respectfully and courteously as you can, move on, and pray that the Spirit of the Lord deal with them accordingly.

Some of the reasons why worshippers break the rules include; ignorance, defiance, forgetfulness, rebellion, etc. It is not up to the doorkeeper to judge or to react based on why they believe the rule was broken; our job is to politely correct them. We must listen to the direction of the Holy Spirit. If the Holy Spirit tells you *not* to speak to someone with regard to an inappropriate behavior, let it go and pray for him or her. Sometimes, people are in a very vulnerable state, and if you approach them with *any* negative statement, you may upset them to the point that they do not come back to the church. That is a situation for which we do not want to be responsible.

There is protocol for the doorkeepers as well as the worshippers. As those who keep the rules of the sanctuary, they must be mindful of their behaviors as well. Remember that we must be an example of proper behavior in the sanctuary. Doorkeepers should be mindful of the following behavior in the sanctuary:

- Doorkeepers should not eat or drink in the sanctuary.
- If they speak it should be in whisper tones and only with regard to keeping order in the sanctuary and not general conversation.
- There should be at least one doorkeeper at the entrance to the sanctuary doors at all times. If a doorkeeper must leave his post, he must make sure that someone is there to relieve him.
- When worshippers go in and out of the sanctuary, hold the door for them. It should be discussed whether all worshippers should be escorted to their seats or only those needing assistance (the elderly, those with small children, etc.).
- If assisting worshippers to find seats, extend your arm, with your hand open, to direct them to the available seat. *Do not point your finger.*
- Escort visiting pastors and their families to the designated area in the sanctuary. (Discuss with your pastor to confirm where they should go.)
- Direct congregation during offering.
- According to your pastor's preference, doorkeepers may be allowed to sit once the sermon begins. One of the doorkeepers should be sitting near the door so that they can hold the door for

worshippers going in and out of the sanctuary during this time.

- Even when sitting, always watch and assist with any movement or activity during the service.
- Movement should be limited during the communion service.
- Keep your eyes on the pastor, as he will direct you if there is any deviation to the usual sanctuary protocol.

The protocol for afternoon services and special services, such as revivals and funerals, should be discussed with the pastor to develop sanctuary rules and doorkeeper protocol for these services. The focus of protocol in the sanctuary is to make sure that worshippers feel comfortable while at the same time keeping order in the sanctuary that is respectful to God. This is accomplished by discouraging unnecessary movement and, at the same time, being sensitive and hospitable to worshippers.

Notes on The Doorkeeper: Protocol in Sanctuary

_____

_____

_____

_____

_____

_____

_____

_____

_____

_____

_____

_____

_____

_____

_____

_____

_____

_____

_____

_____

_____

_____

_____

_____

_____

_____

CHAPTER FIVE

Doorkeepers Preparing for Service

The service responsibilities of a doorkeeper are endless. I will attempt to address some of the more general responsibilities in this chapter.

One of the most important responsibilities of a doorkeeper is timeliness. There are many details to attend to before service begins. You should be at the church fifteen to thirty minutes before service begins, depending on what must be done. If you are unable to be at your post on the assigned day/time, you must notify the head doorkeeper. Ideally, you should notify him or her the day before, but at a minimum one hour before. A doorkeeper must *never* just not show up! It is not only rude, but it is in violation of 1 Corinthians 14:40, which says, "But let all things be done decently and in order.[9]"

Once you arrive at the church, you should check in with the head doorkeeper or whoever is in charge.

---

[9] Thomas Nelson Publishers (1984, 1977) The Holy Bible in the King James Version. Thomas Nelson Publishers, Nashville, TN

The checklist suggested in chapter 3 would be helpful so that everyone knows the general duties that must be performed before service. The following is a sample list of pre-service duties:

- Make sure pews are clean and enough Bibles, hymnbooks, fans, and envelopes are in each section.
- Make sure appropriate lights and heat/air-conditioning are on.
- Make sure you have Kleenex available.
- Be ready to step in and help if shorthanded.
- Check with the head doorkeeper for any special instructions for the service.
- If there are any guest clergy, you should check for any special requirements for them.
- Head doorkeeper should check with the pastor or designated person for any last-minute instructions or changes.

Doorkeepers should meet for unified prayer before manning their posts. Pray for an orderly service, peace, and unity among doorkeepers and whatever the Lord leads you to pray for.

Notes on Doorkeepers Preparing for Service

_____

_____

_____

_____

_____

_____

_____

_____

_____

_____

_____

_____

_____

_____

_____

_____

_____

_____

_____

_____

_____

_____

_____

_____

_____

_____

_____

_____

CHAPTER SIX

Qualities of a Doorkeeper

You must understand that being a doorkeeper is not just a highly visible job in the church where you wear a special uniform and stand around looking important but not doing much. Being a doorkeeper is a gifting and a ministry. The quality of the doorkeeper is like salt that makes everything more palatable and serves as a general preservative against deterioration (Matthew 5:13). Is this your demeanor at the door of your church?

Do you prayerfully work to keep things in order while, at the same time, keeping peace and courtesy? You must resist being judgmental for any reason. Your job is not to judge but to keep order and do it with kindness. A good doorkeeper becomes a landmark to worshippers who learn to depend on them (Matthew 5:14). When a person is not sure of what to do, they look for a doorkeeper. When they need assistance, they look for a doorkeeper. When they need a Kleenex, they will look for a doorkeeper.

Linda J. Williams

As people come in for service, it is the doorkeeper's duty to assist them with seating and to make sure that they are prepared and comfortable for service. Once the service begins, the doorkeeper must focus on God's direction, the pastor, and the people in the sanctuary *all at the same time!* I know that, from my brief experience at the door that this is very difficult to do! If you have never been a doorkeeper, you do not understand the gravity of this time in the service. From the time that the service begins until the benediction, doorkeepers must be totally focused in all these areas.

The pastor (or someone else) may be leading prayer, but a doorkeeper may need to pray with their eyes open. Someone may get up to go out of the sanctuary and you must be able to see them. You must focus on God, so He can tell you if you should stop them or if they have an urgent need and you should help them out quietly. You must keep your eye on the pastor so that, at a time in the service where your church protocol says no one is to be allowed entrance to the sanctuary, you will see him (or her) when they motion for you to let them in. At the same time, you need to see that person who is crying uncontrollably and needs Kleenex. You must see all of these situations, and so much more, so you can properly respond to all of them as the Lord leads you with courtesy and kindness, and at the same time keep order in the sanctuary.

A good doorkeeper is like a lamp. A lamp brings warmth and welcome to all who are in the room[10]. Doorkeepers must have a working knowledge of the Bible. We must love others as God loves us. We cannot know that kind of love if we do not study the Bible and know the Word of God. In addition to our individual Bible study, doorkeepers should attend Bible study and/or Sunday school (2 Timothy 2:15) so that they know the Word of God and are spiritually educated. The spirit of discernment is essential for a good doorkeeper. Without the spirit of discernment, it is difficult to be sensitive to the needs of those in the sanctuary. Without the spirit of discernment, you are like an usher at the movie theater. You follow the rules you are given to enforce, but you are lacking the voice of God saying, "Don't tell that person they are sitting in the wrong place. They just barely made it to church." When you are guided by the spirit of discernment, you will truly be a servant to those in the sanctuary.

Doorkeepers have the difficult task of keeping order and decency while at the same time making those in the sanctuary feel welcome. Nothing assists you in doing that more than a smile! Being a doorkeeper is a gift, and you will know if it is your gift because you will love doing it. No matter how long you are on your feet or how many children you must take to the bathroom, you will love

---

[10] Parrott, L (2002) Serving as a Church Usher. Zondervan, Grand Rapids, MI.

what you do. Because you love what you do, you will smile when you don't feel like it just because you are able to help someone else.

The very character or quality of a doorkeeper is one of a servant. Doorkeepers are not concerned with themselves. Their concern is that everyone in the sanctuary is comfortable and that the holy place of God is kept in order and decency. It is not about you, not about your dress, not about how someone pushed your buttons, not about how you just want to sit down because your feet hurt, and not about how someone disrespected you. A servant takes care of others without regard to themselves. It is a difficult character to build but one that is primary, especially for this position in the church.

Another important component of the doorkeeper quality is appearance. The dress code for the doorkeepers is a topic for which the particulars must be determined by each church and each group of doorkeepers together with their pastor. In today's society, appropriate dress is always a controversial topic, especially when it comes to church. In the case of the doorkeepers, however, this topic should have very little controversy.

The attire of the doorkeepers should be uniform or similar in kind. In many churches, the ladies at the door wear white dresses similar to nurse uniforms while the men wear black suits with white shirts and black ties. On special occasions, the attire may differ slightly, but there should always be a uniform color and appearance.

In addition to the uniformity of the doorkeeper's attire, I must also mention the condition of a doorkeepers' attire. Since your role is somewhat of a disciplinarian with military indications, your attire must be clean and pressed with your name badge straight (and on the right side). Shoes should be shined. (Ladies, wear comfortable shoes). Your appearance should be impeccable (perfect), like that of a soldier.

Female ushers must make sure their uniforms are not too tight, too short, or too revealing. Make sure you wear pantyhose, no matter how warm it is. You should wear minimal makeup and jewelry. The primary reason why doorkeepers are dressed distinctively is so they can be identified quickly. They may also have a lapel pin that says "Doorkeeper" or "Usher" and may have their name. In most Baptist churches, this is how the doorkeepers/ushers are dressed. Other denominations may have the lapel pin, and perhaps all doorkeepers will have matching blazers. Others may have a sash that identifies them as an usher. Some may have nothing that identifies them as an usher. I would suggest that the head doorkeeper meet with the pastor to discuss the attire for the doorkeepers.

The idea of being able to distinguish ushers from other members of the congregation is an important one. Most people, even if they don't attend church on a regular basis, know the role of a doorkeeper (usher). If they are not familiar with ushers in church, they have been to a play, movie, or other venue where doorkeepers are present. They understand that doorkeepers are there to assist, answer questions, help seat them, etc. They assume that they know the rules of the church and can assist with those questions as well. If they can identify who the doorkeepers are, it makes them feel comfortable in knowing that there is someone in close proximity that can assist them if they need it. Sometimes, people are more comfortable calling a doorkeeper over to ask a question or for assistance than asking someone sitting next to them, whether they know them or not. Although the attire of the doorkeeper seems minor, it is a significant part of your position.

One final comment regarding the quality of a doorkeeper is this: you cannot do things in the sanctuary that you are instructing others not to do. Doorkeepers must never chew gum, eat, or drink in the sanctuary. (Mints are okay if discreetly allowed to dissolve in your mouth.) You must always be an example to those whom you serve. You cannot ask them *not* to do what they see you doing or *to* do something that they do not see you doing. As you begin to attain the qualities above, you will find that people will be drawn to you. They will seek you out because of your compassion for them and your passion for your gift as a doorkeeper. The more you give to others, the more they will come to you. You will look like a doorkeeper and have the qualities of a doorkeeper.

Notes on Qualities of Doorkeeper

CHAPTER SEVEN

Attitude of a Doorkeeper

Now that we have discussed the qualities and character of a doorkeeper we should discuss the attitude of a doorkeeper.

An attitude is a manner or disposition and differs from a person's character and qualities. Very simply, attitude is the way you behave toward a person or situation, good or bad. The attitude of a doorkeeper is extremely important because you are the individuals at the doors of the sanctuary. If someone made you mad before you came to church, your attitude may be one of anger. That sends a negative impression to everyone you encounter.

An attitude is a learned behavior and must be controlled by God. The following are some of the attitudes a doorkeeper must strive for:

- having the demeanor of a servant and not a slave; there is a difference.
- being on time for all services and activities.
- doing your work quietly.

- standing tall and capable.
- being optimistic and excited about your church.
- being pleasant in your conversation.
- having a pleasant expression on your face.
- not being judgmental.
- being prayerful.
- being kind.
- being courteous.
- being positive and not negative.
- talking little but observing much.
- making yourself available.

Before you leave home for church, you must make time for meditation and prayer. Pray for those whom you will come in contact with while on your post. Ask God to give you a spirit of discernment as to what to say (or not to say) to each worshipper you encounter. Ask Him for a spirit of love in your heart that shows as you approach each person. Look in the mirror before you leave home. How is your demeanor? Is it pleasant or distant? Listen to yourself as you speak to others. You can hear an attitude in your voice just as others can hear it. Let an attitude of servant hood and grace guide you in performing your duties.

A positive spirit must be cultivated and nurtured to grow. You must first desire a change in your attitude. Once you make up your mind to change you must ask God to show you where to change. Once you know where change is needed, you must make goals for growth. Without goals you will remain stagnant. You will be expecting change but wonder why your attitude is not changing. Allow the Holy Spirit to move you in a direction of change in attitude.

Doorkeepers must encourage and lift up each other. If you see that one of the members of your team looks down or is struggling, go to him or her. Ask if there is anything that you can do. Offer to have prayer with them. If you can assist with some of their duties to take some of the workload from them that day, offer to do so. There should be no dissention within the doorkeeper team. Any issues or disputes must be identified by the head doorkeeper and addressed immediately. I have seen churches where the ushers do not get along and it is noticeable by all, even if you are just a visitor. Proverbs 12:20 states,

> Deceit is in the heart of them that imagine
> evil: but to the counsellors of peace is joy[11].

Doorkeepers must be counsellors of peace and order at all times. You cannot keep the peace with others if there is dissention among you.

I will end this chapter by repeating the definition of attitude: "Manner, disposition, feeling, position, etc., with regard to a person or thing; tendency or orientation, especially of the mind[12]" An attitude, then,

[11] Thomas Nelson Publishers (1984, 1977) The Holy Bible in the King James Version. Thomas Nelson Publishers, Nashville, TN

[12] Copyright © 2015 Dictionary.com, LLC. All rights reserved Dictionary.com, LLC.

can be positive or negative. As doorkeepers, we are not expected to be perfect (or perhaps we are, but we are not). What is expected is that we have a positive attitude, as we have committed to serve the pastor and worshippers of our church.

Linda J. Williams

Notes on Attitude of a Doorkeeper

_____

_____

_____

_____

_____

_____

_____

_____

_____

_____

_____

_____

_____

_____

_____

_____

_____

_____

_____

_____

_____

_____

_____

_____

_____

_____

_____

_____

_____

CHAPTER EIGHT

The Spirit of Hospitality

Hospitality is the friendly reception and treatment of guests or strangers. In our churches, we as believers should extend a spirit of hospitality to everyone. As a doorkeeper, we *must* extend the spirit of love and hospitality to everyone who enters the doors of the church.

In the secular world, this role would be similar to a doorman or concierge at a hotel. If you have ever stayed at an upscale hotel, dined at an upscale restaurant, or attended a theater performance, remember how the hospitality staff treated you. Whether it was a concierge, waiter, or usher, they were ready to meet your every need with kindness, respect, and eagerness to make sure that your experience at their establishment was a pleasant one. Regardless to the kind of day they are having personally these persons are paid to show the utmost kindness and courtesy. They are expected to do whatever is necessary to assist guests in their hotel with any issue that is brought to them. Doorkeepers are not paid to show the utmost kindness and do whatever is necessary to assist those who come to worship in their church. We are given so much more. Christ gave His life so that our sins would be forgiven and so that we could dedicate our lives in service and obedience to God. That is worth so much more than a monetary salary, yet so many who are keepers of the doors of the sanctuaries of God do so without regard for the seriousness of this position. The spirit of hospitality must prevail if we are to be effective doorkeepers.

Some churches have persons who are designated greeters. Their job is to smile and greet worshippers as they enter the church. The job of a greeter, though important, does not take the place of the doorkeeper.

If, in fact, you do have greeters in your church, they are probably the first people to give a welcome greeting to those coming in. Then the churchgoers come to the doors of the sanctuary where the doorkeepers stand. We must also have that hospitable greeting for those who come in. If we do not, this sends mixed messages and people wonder whether or not they are truly welcome. Some of the traits of the spirit of hospitality include the following:

- greeting each person with a genuine smile filled with the love of God;
- greeting *every* person you make eye contact with as they come through the door;
- saying good-morning;
- Not asking people how they are unless you have time to listen to them!;
- learning the names of members and those who attend frequently, because people like to hear their name;

- anticipating the needs of attendees and doing whatever you can to make them feel comfortable and welcome;

- focusing on what is going on in the sanctuary and being ready to provide assistance (people in wheelchairs, people with babies and children, etc.);

- seeing the Spirit of God in you and in everything that you do;

- thinking about the heart and character of your pastor (People look at you and your behavior, but they judge your pastor and everyone in the church by how you behave.);

- being compassionate.

Guests must be treated with a special measure of hospitality. Guests may be visiting from another church or they may be seeking a church home. Your behavior toward a guest may determine if they return to your church or *any* church. Think of a guest in your church as a guest in your home. Although you did not invite them, God sent them, and He expects us to treat them with courtesy.

Finally, be ye all of one mind, having compassion one of another, love as brethren, be pitiful, and be courteous.
—1 Peter 3:8[13]

---

[13] Thomas Nelson Publishers (1984, 1977) The Holy Bible in the King James Version. Thomas Nelson Publishers, Nashville, TN

Notes on the Spirit of Hospitality

CHAPTER NINE

Goals for Growth

(Changing Your Attitude)

Setting goals for any reason requires focus. You must first know why you are setting goals, and then you must decide what goals need to be put in place. Finally, you must prioritize for execution. You must ask God for a willingness in your heart to change. God will then begin to show you where and how to focus.

The following are some areas on which to focus for growth in your relationship with God to be a more Spirit-filled doorkeeper:

- Work unto the Lord to please Him in your duties (Colossians 3:17, 23).
- Be filled with the Word of God (Proverbs 4:20–22).
- Be strong in your faith (Romans 10:17).
- Be led by the Spirit of God (Romans 8:14).

- Speak faith-filled words, believing what you say (Mark 11:23–24).
- You must control your tongue (James 3:2–8, Ephesians 4:29–32).
- You must be free of backbiting (Psalm 15:1–3).
- You must be filled with the compassion of Jesus (Matthew 9:36).
- You must walk in the power of God so that you will not hurt or be hurt (Luke 10:19).
- You must walk in obedience (Jeremiah 7:23, Isaiah 1:19–20, Colossians 3:22).
- You must be faithful (Luke 16:10).
- You must be dependable (1 John 2:5–6).
- You must treat others better than you treat yourself (Romans 12:10, Philippians 2:3).
- You must be free of envy and strife (Proverbs 14:30).
- You must always be willing to forgive (Matthew 6:14–15, Luke 6:37–38).
- You must be a *doer* of the Word and not just quote the Word (James 1:22–25).
- You must stay "built up" in the Spirit (Jude 20–21).

We must continually attain growth in our walk but strive for perfection. Each of these goals is validated by Scripture to emphasize the importance of growing in each area according to the Word of God.

To attain a goal you must look at the overall goal and then set specific tasks to get you there. Prayerfully review each of the goals above. Determine which ones are areas of weakness for you. Pray and ask God to prioritize these areas or others. Keep a journal so that you can keep track of your triumphs (and failures). As you become victorious in an area you can move on to the next area. Don't become complacent in those areas of growth as they can return. As you work on new areas you must continue to pray and thank God for the growth areas as well. Your attitude as a doorkeeper must exemplify that of a servant in all that you do.

Notes on Goals for Growth

_____

_____

_____

_____

_____

_____

_____

_____

_____

_____

_____

_____

_____

_____

_____

_____

_____

_____

_____

_____

_____

_____

_____

_____

CHAPTER TEN

The Passion to Be a Doorkeeper

In this final chapter, I want to provide you with some questions for reflection.

1. Why do you want to be a doorkeeper?
2. Did you volunteer to be a doorkeeper? Why?
3. When you agreed to take the job, did you know what it involved?
4. Are your aware that you must be a servant to others?
5. Do you like interacting with people? Children?
6. Are you willing to be a courteous, caring servant?
7. What comments, if any, have others made to you (positively or negatively) about your job as a doorkeeper?
8. Do you still want to be a doorkeeper?
9. Are you willing to pray and ask God to show you the areas where change is needed?
10. Are you willing to change?
11. What do you need to change?
12. Can you change?

The above questions are very serious and must be answered carefully and honestly by every doorkeeper. First Corinthians 12:1–12 states,

> Now concerning spiritual gifts, brethren, I would not have you ignorant. Ye know that ye were Gentiles, carried away unto these dumb idols, even as ye were led. Wherefore I give you to understand, that no man speaking by the Spirit of God calleth Jesus accursed: and that no man can say that Jesus is the Lord, but by the Holy Ghost. Now there are diversities of gifts, but the same Spirit. And there are differences of administrations, but the same Lord. And there are diversities of operations, but it is the same God which worketh all in all.
>
> But the manifestation of the Spirit is given to every man to profit withal.
>
> For to one is given by the Spirit the word of wisdom; to another the word of knowledge by the same Spirit; To another faith by the same Spirit; to another the gifts of healing by the same Spirit; To another the working of miracles; to another prophecy; to another discerning of spirits; to another divers kinds of tongues; to another the interpretation of tongues: But

all these worketh that one and the selfsame Spirit, dividing to every man severally as he will[14].

I share the above Scripture because God has blessed each of us with a gift. The gift may evolve or change slightly, but it is still the same primary gift. For example, I have come to understand that my gift is the gift of encouragement, as well as knowledge for the ministry of courtesy as stated in 1 Peter 3:8. There is a connection with these gifts, which took some time for God to reveal to me.

As my gift expanded from teaching to writing, I came to the understanding that the area of the use of my gift may change, but it is always connected to the area of encouragement and courtesy. It is one small Scripture, but a very important gift; as are all of our gifts from God.

I share this knowledge with you because we have all received a gift from God. You too must cultivate that gift so that it will grow and become strong for the glory of God. Your gift is usually that thing that you have a passion for. You may not even realize you have a passion for it; you just know that when you are doing it, you are filled with joy. One of the definitions of passion is: "The object of such a fondness or desire.[15]" It means that when you are doing this particular thing, no matter how complicated or difficult it may be, you totally enjoy it.

---

[14] Thomas Nelson Publishers (1984, 1977) The Holy Bible in the King James Version. Thomas Nelson Publishers, Nashville, TN

[15] Copyright ©2015 Dictionary.com, LLC. All rights reserved. Dictionary.com, LLC.

You love it so much you would do it for free, even though people may pay you to do it. We should all know what our gift from God is because that is our purpose for being here. If you do not know or, are not sure, there are many spiritual gift questionnaires that can help you. The one that I recommend is *Finding Your Spiritual Gifts* by C. Peter Wagner. The website to order the questionnaire is www. gospellight.com.

So how are the above paragraphs connected to being a doorkeeper? If your gift is to be a doorkeeper, you will know it. It will be a passion for you. Being a servant to the people of God will not make you feel like you are being taken advantage of or like the position is beneath you.

You will find joy in helping the worshippers who come to your church on Sunday morning. Cleaning out the pews will not feel like drudgery to you. You will not be upset if one of the doorkeepers doesn't show up and you are asked to take their post at the last minute. You will have a genuine smile for the people of God as they come in. You will have a prayer on your lips for them and will not judge them because of how they are dressed, how they may smell, or if they are rude to you.

As you grow in your gift as a doorkeeper, the level of your spirit of discernment will increase. You will become more confident and know when to speak, when to pray, when to move, and when to be still. You will understand what the pastor's facial expressions and gestures mean and move without hesitation. You will anticipate the movement of worshippers and be able to approach them to either direct or assist them at a moment's notice. You will do all of this and be joyful and grateful to God for the gift He has deposited in you.

If, however, the above situations are unpleasant to you and difficult for you to react to or understand, perhaps the position of doorkeeper is not for you. I mentioned earlier in the book that I knew after the first two Sundays at the door that this was definitely *not* my calling. I understood that it was only temporary and that, as etiquette officer, my primary job was to keep order in the sanctuary, not to pretend to be a doorkeeper. If you discover that being a doorkeeper is truly not your calling, talk to the head doorkeeper and your pastor if necessary. Time is too short to continue in a ministry that is not your gift. Ephesians 5:15–16 states,

> Pay careful attention, then, to how you walk— not as unwise people but as wise—making the most of the time, because the days are evil[16].

We do not know how much time we have left to fulfill the purpose God has given us; some have been given more time than others (Psalms 90:10). We must be about our job, our purpose, and our Father's business. We must do it with obedience, wisdom, and passion. We must not worry about being embarrassed or that we might be

---

[16] Thomas Nelson Publishers (1984, 1977) The Holy Bible in the King James Version. Thomas Nelson Publishers, Nashville, TN

criticized or ridiculed. We must follow God's direction prayerfully and explicitly so that we can do the job God created us to do.

As Christians, we should know that each of us must be diligent about prayerfully perfecting our gift. If we realize we are cultivating the wrong gift, we must prayerfully ask God to redirect our steps to our gift. Don't be embarrassed; just move as God directs you.

In the introduction, I explained how this book prayerfully came into being. I want to end by sharing with you the statement that God puts people in your life for a "season" to guide you into the plan He has for you. The seed for the first book I wrote on church etiquette in 2009 was planted by my former pastor, who is now deceased. One Sunday morning during service, he literally looked at me and said, "You should write a book on church etiquette." My current pastor planted the seed for this book by showing me that the training manual that I prayerfully put together for our doorkeepers should be published as a book so that other churches could gain knowledge for their doorkeepers. When I wrote the first book, I had no visions of writing another book; but God did.

The above testimony leads to my "Doorkeeper's Challenge" for you. If you have been chosen by God or your pastor, or both, to be a doorkeeper, don't back away from the commitment. If after reading all that is contained in this book, your passion to be a doorkeeper is stronger than ever, I challenge you to spend time in prayer and meditation so that God can mold you into the doorkeeper He expects you to be. There are many doorkeepers, but each doorkeeper has a particular ministry, character, and purpose. Those on your team of doorkeepers were brought together by God for His purpose in your church.

Think about a job that you really wanted or an idea that you wanted to make a reality. Remember how diligently and passionately you worked toward that goal? We must apply that same zeal and passion (or more) to the gift and purpose God has deposited in us. No one else can do the job that God created us to do. If we do not complete it, it will remain undone and people may suffer as a result. The more difficult the task is that God gives you to do, the greater the reward when you are obedient. Romans 12:6–8 states,

> Having then gifts differing according to the grace that is given to us, whether prophecy, let us prophesy according to the proportion of faith; or ministry, let us wait on our ministering: or he that teacheth, on teaching; or he that exhorteth, on exhortation: he that giveth, let him do it with simplicity; he that ruleth, with diligence; he that sheweth mercy, with cheerfulness[17].

---

[17] Thomas Nelson Publishers (1984, 1977) The Holy Bible in the King James Version. Thomas Nelson Publishers, Nashville, TN

For those who read this book hoping to gain insight into the ministry of being a doorkeeper, I pray that you have found at least one piece of information to guide you in this important role. I recommend that you prayerfully reread this handbook again for clarity and direction. Let God show you the areas in which you shine and the areas that you must give to Him for growth and perfection. Make notes on the "Notes" pages so that will become your personalized handbook. Then you will be able to stand at the doors of your sanctuary as Shallum, son of Kore, in 1 Chronicles 9:19.

May the Spirit of the Lord be with you as you stand at the door of the house of the Lord.

Notes on The Passion to Be a Doorkeeper

_____

_____

_____

_____

_____

_____

_____

_____

_____

_____

_____

_____

_____

_____

_____

_____

_____

_____

_____

_____

_____

_____

_____

_____

_____

Notes on Passion to Be a Doorkeeper

Notes on Passion to Be a Doorkeeper

_____

_____

_____

_____

_____

_____

_____

_____

_____

_____

_____

_____

_____

_____

_____

_____

_____

_____

_____

_____

_____

_____

_____

_____

_____

_____

CPSIA information can be obtained at www.ICGtesting.com
Printed in the USA
LVOW10s0354020915

452503LV00001B/12/P